CO

see it		2
buy it		6
watch it	entertainment	26
taste it	places to eat and drink	38
know it	practical information	48
directory	hotel listings and more	56
speak it	and index	62

Map references are denoted in the text by ❶ North Chicago
❷ South Chicago ❸ In the Loop ❹ Around Chicago ❺ Chicago Transit

chicago places to see

Sprawled for miles along the side of Lake Michigan and bisected by the Chicago river, this amazing city is home to some of the world's most innovative architecture, incomparable museums and galleries, and a thriving cosmopolitan community. While suburbs such as Oak Park burst with fine Queen Anne and Prairie School architecture, the center is crowded with landmark skyscrapers, testament to the genius of the architects who have rebuilt the city since the Great Fire of 1871. This ongoing regeneration lends to the US's third largest city a vibrant new dynamic, which, happily for those who visit, has lost none of its innate Midwestern geniality, courtesy, and charm. This really is the big city with the heart of a small town.

see it places to see

Sights

Adler Planetarium & Astronomy Museum ❷ 1M

Built in the 1930s, the Adler was the first modern planetarium in the western world. It now houses a renowned astronomical collection and the fabulous StarRider Theater, a virtual space experience in which the visitor can explore everything from the surface of Mars to the outer reaches of the universe. Designed by architect Ernest Grunsfeld, grandfather of the NASA astronaut John Grunsfeld, each of the 12 corners of the building is decorated with a sign of the zodiac. *Adm. Free Mon, Tue late Sep-Feb. Open Mon-Fri 9.30am-4.30pm, Sat-Sun 9am-4.30pm. Museum Campus: 1300 S Lake Shore Dr, T: 312 922 7827, www.adlerplanetarium.org*

Art Institute of Chicago ❷ 3J/❸

This neo-classical building, built for the World's Fair in 1893, shelters an

The domed façade of the Adler Planetarium

A lion stands proud outside the Art Institute

unmissable art collection that spans 50 centuries and several continents. Well known for its Impressionist and Post-Impressionist collections, exhibiting fine works by artists such as Monet, Degas, and Van Gogh, it also has remarkable galleries of Egyptian, Chinese, Asian, medieval, modern, and Renaissance art and artifacts. Visit the temporary exhibitions, installations, and lectures. *Free on Tue. Open Mon-Wed & Fri 10.30am-4.30pm, Thu 10.30am-8pm, Sat & Sun 10am-5pm. 111 S Michigan Ave, T: 312 443 3600, www.artic.edu*

Bahá'í House of Worship ❹

The Bahá'í Faith is the world's secondmost widespread independent religion and this lovely temple is one of only seven major houses of worship world-wide. Designed in the 1920s by Louis Bourgeois, it has to be the North Shore's most impressive structure. A nonagon, it is symbolic

Dome of the Bahá'í House of Worship

The elaborate Buckingham Fountain in Grant Park

of the Bahá'í faith, which promotes understanding and harmony between all people. The temple has an exquisite quartz-covered dome that soars to 135 feet, and quotations from 19th-century founder Bahá'u'lláh adorn the nine alcoves and entrance arches. Since 1953, more than five million people have visited this peaceful haven and its lovely gardens, which boast marvelous views over Lake Michigan. *Gardens and auditorium open daily 7am-6.30pm, Visitors Center open daily 10am-5pm. 112 Linden Ave, Wilmette (one hour north of city; last stop on Purple Line). T: 847 853 2300, www.us.bahai.org*

Buckingham Fountain ❷ 3K

Designed in 1927 by Edward Bennett, this pink marble fountain represents Lake Michigan; the four seahorses at each corner symbolizing Wisconsin, Illinois, Indiana, and Michigan, the four states that touch the lake. One of the largest fountains in the world, it has a capacity of 1.5

see it

The decorative Tiffany Dome in the Chicago Cultural Center

million gallons. Once every hour the computer-controlled water spurts an impressive 135 feet! *Open daily Apr-Oct. Columbus Dr at Congress Pkwy.*

Chicago Cultural Center ❷ 3J/❸

The city's former main library, this neo-classical building dates from 1897 and is now home to the Department of Cultural Affairs and its wide range of visual, performing, and literary arts programs. Elegant and opulent, it is famed for its two spectacular stained-glass domes (one by Tiffany), sparkling mosaics, and intricate ceilings. Inside, there are rooms modeled on the Doge's Palace, Venice; the Palazzo Vecchio, Florence; and the Acropolis, Athens. *Free. Open Mon-Thu 8am-7pm, Fri 8am-6pm, Sat 9am-6pm, Sun 10am-6pm. 78 E Washington St, T: 312 744 6630, egov.cityofchicago.org*

Chicago Historical Society ❶ 4D

This museum and research center is the ultimate authority on the ongoing story of Chicago and Illinois. Home to more than 20 million artifacts and documents, it covers pioneer life, the Great Fire of 1871, the history of Chicago neighborhoods, and the period between the Declaration of Independence in 1776 and the Civil War in 1861. *Adm. Open Mon-Sat*

Full of Hot Air

It may seem obvious that Chicago should be known as the 'Windy City,' with the wind sometimes coming off the lake in 40-mph gusts. In fact, the tag refers to the 'long-winded' *braggadocio*, or arrogant behavior, for which local politicians became renowned at the 1893 World's Columbian Exhibition. The name stuck, even while everything from umbrellas to hats continues to blow away.

9.30am-4.30pm, Sun 12 noon-5pm. 1601 N Clark St at W North Ave, T: 312 642 4600, www.chicagohistory.org

Daley Civic Center ❷ 4J/❸

Picasso's untitled, unpainted 50-ft Cubist sculpture is a focal point of this open-air gallery. Weighing 162 tons and made of corrosive, tensile, self-weathering steel, it represents a woman's head. To see the head, stand behind the sculpture at 'five o'clock.' *50 W Washington Ave.*

Surreal Picasso sculpture in Daley Plaza

Lloyd Wright's Robie House

DuSable Museum of African-American History ❷ 6N

The first museum devoted solely to African-American history in the US, this museum offers exhibits, film screenings, lectures, tours, concerts, and theater programs. *Adm. Free Sun. Mon-Sat 10am-5pm, Sun 12pm-5pm. 740 E 56th Pl, T: 773 947 0600, www.dusablemuseum.org*

Field Museum of Natural History ❷ 2M

A center of exhibition and research excellence featuring displays on nature, dinosaurs, and Pacific cultures. Its most famous exhibit is 'Sue,' a tyrannosaurus named after Susan Hendrickson, who discovered the skeleton in 1990. *Free Tue. Open daily 9am-5pm. Museum Campus: 1400 S Lake Shore Dr, T: 312 922 9410, www.fieldmuseum.org*

An elephant in the atrium at the Field Museum

Frederick C Robie House ❷ 6N

One of the finest of the 75 buildings designed by Frank Lloyd Wright, this 1909 Prairie-style house features 174 exquisite, decorative art glass windows and doors. *Adm. Tours Mon-Fri 11am-3pm, Sat & Sun 11am-3.30pm. 5757 S Woodlawn Ave, T: 773 834 1847, www.wrightplus.org*

Harold Washington Library ❷ 4K

At 756,640 square feet, this is the world's largest library. Constructed in 1987 in honor of the city's first black mayor, the design is neo-classical with four-corner ornamentation of owls perched in foliage (see p.54). Free. Mon-Thu 9am-7pm, Fri & Sat 9am-5pm, Sun 1-5pm. 400 S State St, T: 312 747 4999, www.chipublib.org

John Hancock Tower

Illinois Institute of Technology ❹

Famed for technology, engineering, and architecture, the IIT is home to 22 buildings designed by Ludwig Mies van der Rohe. The jewel is the Crown Hall, whose interior consists of one large, column-free room. The roof is hung from exposed steel trusses bridging the building's depth. Also check out the Koolhaas-designed Campus Center: the L-train goes right through the building. 3360 S State St, T: 312 567 3000.

James R Thompson Center ❷ 4I/❸

This Helmut Jahn design is a glass-enclosed steel structure with a curved and sloping façade. It was completed in 1985 as the State of Illinois building and renamed in 1993 for the then governor. Free. Open Mon-Fri 8am-5pm. 100 W Randolph St, T: 312 814 6660.

John Hancock Tower ❶ 3F

After the Sears Tower, this is the highest observation point in Chicago, boasting an outdoor Skywalk 1,000 feet above the Magnificent Mile (see pp.18-20).

Lincoln Park Lagoon and Café Brauer

Other attractions include soundscapes, talking telescopes (in four languages); and Windows of Chicago, technology that allows you to 'tour' more than 80 attractions. Adm. Open daily 9am-11pm. 875 N Michigan Ave, T: 312 751 3681, www.hancock-observatory.com

Lincoln Park ❶ 4D

Lincoln Park is one of many urban oases conceived by Daniel H Burnham and Frederick Law Olmsted to bring the country to the city. Together these form Chicago's park system, known as the 'emerald necklace.' In Lincoln's 1,200 lake-front acres, you'll find the Zoo, home to more than 1,000 animal species; and the Conservatory, a jungle of tropical palms, ferns and orchids. *Free. Conservatory: open daily 9am-5pm. 2391 N Stockton Dr, T: 312 742 7736. Zoo: open daily 9am-4.30pm winter, Mon-Fri 9am-6pm, Sat-Sun 9am-7pm summer. 2200 N Cannon Dr, T: 312 742 2000, www.lpzoo.org*

Magnificent Mile on North Michigan Ave ❶ 3G & p.18

The city's premier shopping street is also site of some of Chicago's finest modern architecture. It starts at Michigan Ave Bridge (3I), which spans the Chicago river, and sweeps up past the Wrigley Building and the Tribune Tower (*see p.13*), the swanky Hotel Inter-Continental (*see p.57*), and chic designer stores (*see pp.18-20*). Northward from here is Chicago Place Shopping Center (3G), the Old Water Tower (*see p.11*) and Pumping Station, the shopping opportunity that is Water Tower Place (*see p.20*), and the John Hancock Tower (*see left*), which stands opposite the Gothic-Revival Fourth Presbyterian Church. *866 N Michigan Ave, T: 312 787 4570.*

Millennium Park ❷ 3J/❸

A must see! Located in downtown Chicago, and the newest City of Chicago Park, this is an unprecedented center for world-class art, music, architecture and landscape design. Completed in 2004, it features a Frank Gehry-designed band shell. Home to summer concerts. *401 W Randolph btn Michigan Ave & Columbus Dr. www.millenniumpark.org*

Millennium Pk's Cloud Gate ('Bean') Sculpture

Checagou! Checagou!

It took a while to settle on Chicago's name. The first spelling was credited to local Native American tribes who populated the land near the Chicago river in the 1600s. When the Haitian fur trader Jean Baptiste Point du Sable established a small settlement here in 1779, he called it 'Eschikagou.' Some say the word means 'wild onions,' which grew abundantly in the region. Others say it means 'strong' or 'great,' which, so legend has it, Du Sable knew the city would one day be. As the first settler, he is credited as the city's founder.

Monadnock Building ❷ 4K/❸

Built in 1891, the 16-story north part of this building was one of Chicago's first skyscrapers. With its monumental, six-foot-thick masonry walls, the design by architects Burnham & Root was bold at a time when ornamental architecture was paramount. The south part, designed by Holabird and Roche, has a steel frame covered in terracotta. *53 W Jackson Blvd.*

Museum of Contemporary Art ❶3G
Although the emphasis is on temporary shows, there is a strong, permanent collection here showing post-war work. Displays include 40s' and 50s' Surrealism, 60s' minimalism, conceptual art, and photography since 1960. There are regular live performances in the 300-seat theater. *Adm. Open Tue 10am-8pm (free from 5pm), Wed-Sun 10am-5pm.*

> **Extreme Measures**
> At 31.6 feet, Longmeadow is Chicago's shortest street. The longest street is Western Avenue, which stretches 23.5 miles through town.

220 E Chicago Ave, T: 312 280 2660, www.mcachicago.org

Museum of Science & Industry ❷5N
Well worth a visit, this 350,000-square-foot building, formerly the 1893 World Fair's Palace of Fine Arts,

The neo-classical Museum of Science and Industry

Ferris Wheel at Navy Pier

hosts more than 800 interactive exhibits, including a World War II German submarine, an acoustically perfect whispering gallery, the Apollo 8 spacecraft, a coal mine replica, and a baby chick hatchery. There is also a domed, 72-ft Omnimax Theater. *Adm. Open Mon-Sat 9.30am-5.30pm, Sun 11am-5.30pm (restricted hours Nov-Dec). E 57th St & Lake Shore Dr, T: 773 684 1414, www.msichicago.org*

Navy Pier ❶1H
This revamped naval base is the city's most visited attraction and boasts a 150-ft ferris wheel modeled after the one built for Chicago's 1893 Exposition. Other attractions include

lake cruises, an open-air theater, IMAX films, restaurants, and shops. *Adm. Open daily. 600 E Grand Ave, T: 312 595 7437, www.navypier.com*

Newberry Library ❶ 4F

Chicago's research library boasts a collection of 1.5 million titles, five million manuscript pages, and 300,000 historic maps. It specializes in history, literature, and genealogy

The Old Water Tower in front of the Hancock

Curving staircase at the historic Rookery Building (see p.12)

through to cartography, Native American life, and music theory. *Free. Open Tue-Thu 10am-6pm, Fri & Sat 9am-5pm. 60 Walton St, T: 312 943 9090, www.newberry.org*

The Old Water Tower ❶ 3G

Completed in 1869, William W Boyington's elaborate Gothic folly was one of the few buildings to survive the 1871 Great Fire. It stands 154 ft above the street and is home to the City Gallery and the Lookingglass Theatre *(see p.35)*. Next door, a pumping station built in 1866 clears 250 million gallons of water a day. *Adm. Open Mon-Sat 10am-6.30pm, Sun 10am-5pm. 806 N Michigan Ave, T: 773 477 5845.*

Oak Park ❹

A tranquil suburban setting for some of Chicago's finest architecture, chief of which is the gaggle of 25 builds by Frank Lloyd Wright, including his Home and Studio, the Arthur Heurtley House, and Unity Temple. Oak Park was the birthplace of Ernest Hemingway – his elegant Victorian home is full of grand 19th-

century furnishings.
T: 708 524 7800, www.oprf.com

Oriental Institute Museum ❷ 6O
Look no further for antiquities from Egypt, Persia, Mesopotamia, and Anatolia. *Free. Open Tue, Thu-Sat 10am-6pm, Wed 10am-8.30pm, Sun 12-6pm. 1155 E 58th St (Univ. of Chicago Campus), T: 773 702 9514, www.oi.uchicago.edu*

The Sears Tower peers over Monroe Harbor

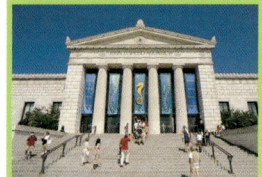

Steps up to the Shedd Aquarium

The Rookery Building ❷ 4J/❸
This muscular Chicago landmark was built in 1888 by the prestigious firm Burnham & Root just prior to their design for the Monadnock Building (*see p.9*). See the south façade for the load-bearing technology paving the way for the modern skyscraper. Frank Lloyd Wright redesigned the two-tiered court inside the entrance in 1907. *209 S La Salle St.*

Sears Tower Skydeck ❷ 5J/❸
At 103 floors above the Loop (*see p.21*), the Sears Tower boasts the highest indoor observation deck in the world – for now. Viewing spans 50 miles in all directions – north to Wisconsin, east to Michigan, and south and west to Illinois farmland.

Other attractions include interactive displays and a multi-media elevator ride. *Adm. Open daily 10am-10pm May-Sep, Oct-Apr 10am-8pm. 223 S Wacker Dr, T: 312 875 9696, www.theskydeck.com*

Ceres-ous Money
The world's largest futures and options exchange trades corn, soybean, wheat, and treasury notes in the 1929 Holabird & Root (❷ 3K/❸) Board of Trade building. It is topped with an image of Ceres, goddess of grain, and has a dramatic three-story lobby. *Free. 141 W Jackson, T: 312 435 3625, www.cbot.com*

buy it places to shop

buy it

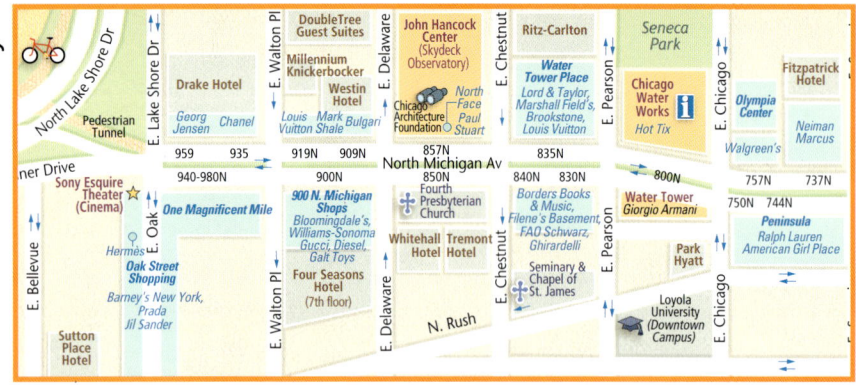

Magnificent Mile

To stroll this boulevard is to settle the matter: it truly is shopping paradise. Here you will find a gleaming array of exclusive and minimalist designer shops and cool restaurants, with all the glittery mainstays like Saks Fifth Avenue, Armani, Louis Vuitton, Neiman Marcus, Burberry, Gucci, and Tiffany & Co as well as the newest additions such as MaxMara, Polo Ralph Lauren, and The Gap. Don't miss Water Tower Place (see p.20) for seven floors of absolute shopping joy.

Apple Store see above
Constantly abuzz with activity and happy mac lovers, this interactive venue doubles as an Internet cafe. Free presentations, and workshops are featured with rotating themes on topics such as digital photography and music. *679 North Michigan Ave, T: 312 981 4104, www.apple.com*

Bloomingdale's ❶ 3F, and above
This is the Midwest's flagship store, which rivals its New York kith and kin. Everything you ever dreamed about buying and a whole lot more.

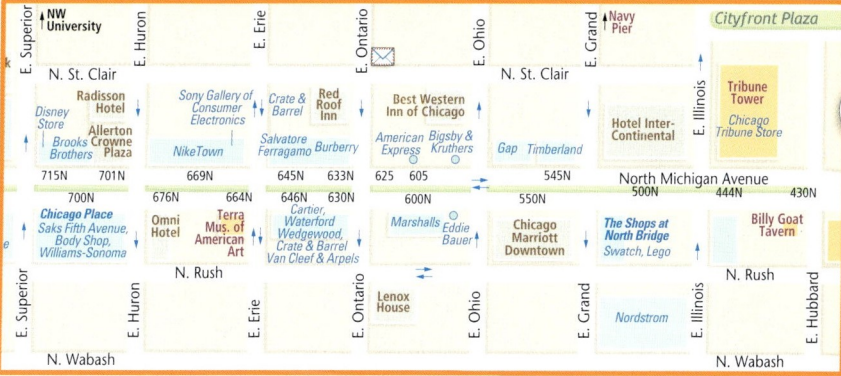

Designer gear and accessories of the highest order. *900 N Michigan Ave, T: 312 440 4460, bloomingdales.com*

Brookstone see above
Selection of up-market necessities for the traveler, gardener, or fitness fanatic or just for the home. *Water Tower Place, 835 N Michigan Ave, T: 312 943 6356, www.brookstone.com*

N Michigan Ave lit up for Christmas

buy it

Bloomie's in the mall at 900 N Michigan

Crate & Barrel ❶ 3G & p.19
A feast for the eyes! The Crate & Barrel collections of housewares and furniture are creatively arranged in a crisp, clean, architectural setting designed to make you visualize how it will all feel in your home. *646 N Michigan, T: 312 787 5900, www.crateandbarrel.com*

Tax on Your Shopping
Sales tax for Illinois is at 9 percent but if you have items shipped out of state, there is no charge.

Ermenegildo Zegna ❶ 3G
This men's boutique boasts the best in fabrics and in cut. *645 N Michigan Ave, T: 312 587 9660.*

Garrett Popcorn Shop p.19
This postage-stamp sized shop has been around since 1949. There is usually a line snaking along Michigan Avenue to buy helpings of their highly rated popcorn. Just ask for the Downtown Mix. *670 N Michigan Ave, T: 312 944 2630, www.garrettpopcorn.com*

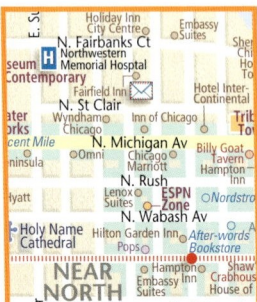

You're My Main Mall
The malls of Michigan Avenue are the gilded heart of Chicago's shopping experience.

900 N Michigan Ave p.18
Shops, galleries, restaurants, and hotels. *T: 312 915 3916. www.shop900.com*

Chicago Place p.19
Fifty stylish stores on eight levels, including Saks Fifth Avenue. *700 N Michigan Ave, T: 312 266 7710.*

Water Tower Place ❶ 3G & p.18
Big-name gloss. *835 N Michigan Ave, T: 312 440 3165. www.shopwatertower.com*

Gucci p.18
The main Chicago showcase for this upmarket but ready-to-wear designs for women, plus accessories and shoes for both sexes. *900 N Michigan Ave, T: 312 664 5504, www.gucci.com*

Other Areas

Andersonville ❹

An interesting mix of old and new in terms of architecture and residents. The once traditionally Swedish enclave now shares its real estate with new, colorful residents of many races, from Japanese to Persian and Andean. Check out the Landmark (*5301 N Clark St, T: 773 728 5301*), a multi-level retail co-op and take a pit stop in the Swedish Bakery (*5348 N Clark St, T: 773 561 8919*) for forbidden heavenly no-nos.

Bucktown & Wicker Park ❹

The boundary lines of this growing funky community are fluid – just follow the trendies. The hub is roughly North and Damen Aves. Lots of young designers have set up shop here. For literary nourishment, visit Myopic Books for used bargains. *1564 N Milwaukee, T: 773 862 4882, www.myopicbookstore.com*

Lincoln Park ❶ 4A-4D

Trendy-funky well describes this firmly established hub of fashion; with bookstores and specialty shops on every strip. Located west of the park, it is loaded with charming stores like hip clothing boutique Shop Girl + Swell (*1206 W. Webster*), Saturday's Child (*2146 N Halsted Ave*), and home-furnishing supremo Crate & Barrel (*646 N Michigan Ave*).

The Loop ❷ 4I-4J/❸

The nerve center of the city, the loop is a mix of old Chicago, like Marshall Field's, a dollop of the new, and affordable chains like Filene's Basement (*830 N Michigan Ave*). The area is bordered by the L (*see p.52*),

> **Shopping Made Easy**
> Feeling all shopped out? Put the task in the hands of your very own personal shopper. At no charge Marshall Field's (*see p.23*) and Saks Fifth Avenue at Chicago Place (*see box, left*) will advise, select, wrap, and ship your parcels to any destination in the world.

Shoppers along Oak Street

which loops around its confines for easy access to the shops.

Oak Street ❶ 3F & p.18

Ultimo, Prada, Barney's, Jil Sander, Betsey Johnson, and Nicole Miller are just a few of the designers to dot this street. If you're not in a spending frame of mind, the people-watching is just as edifying.

South Loop ❷ 4L-4M

The South Loop is all quaint charm. The lofts and warehouses have been taken over and renovated by rich young professionals who can walk to

buy it

Fascinating collectibles in Salvage One

work in the Loop. At the same time the outdoor markets (*see p.24*) are experiencing a rebirth.

Antiques

Salvage One ❹
Wonderful and eccentric store crammed full of reclaimed ancient stone bas-reliefs, brass wall hangings, marble fireplaces, sundials, and stained glass. *1840 W Hubbard St, T: 312 733 0098, www.salvageone.com*

Books & Maps

In addition to the stores listed below, there are also several branches of Borders and Barnes & Noble scattered around the city.

The Savvy Traveller ❷ 3K
Everything for the sussed traveler, from games and inspirational books to enthrall the kids to travel guides and camping, biking, and hiking equipment for outdoors enthusiasts. *310 S Michigan Ave, T: 312 913 9800, www.thesavvytraveller.com*

Transitions Bookplace ❶ 6D
A New-Age mecca for books, tapes, and Eastern paraphernalia, with an hospitable café. Regular lectures by gurus such as Deepak Chopra. *1000 W North Ave, T: 312 951 7323, www.transitionsbookplaqce.com*

Women & Children First ❹
Just like the name says, this bookstore specializes in women's, children's, and feminist literature. There are regular evening readings. *5233 N Clark St, T: 773 769 9299, www.womenandchildrenfirst.com*

Candy

Margie's Candies ❹
This old-time Chicago ice cream parlor is filled with gaudy knick-knacks that would be at home in your grandmother's house. *1960 N Western St, T: 773 384 1035.*

Department Stores

Carson Pirie Scott & Co ❷ 4J/❸
The main store of several branches, with quality merchandise housed in architect Louis Sullivan's greatest masterpiece of design. *1 S State St, T: 312 641 7000, www.carsons.com*

The famous clock at Marshall Field's

Designer boutique Jil Sander

Lord & Taylor ❷ 4l/❸
A reasonably priced Chicago department store; not cutting-edge in design terms but with a reputation for well-priced and well-made clothing for men, women, and children. *Water Tower Place, 835 N Michigan Ave, T: 312 787 7400, www.lordandtaylor.com*

Marshall Field's ❷ 4l/❸
Possibly the most up-market department store in the US and certainly Chicago's preeminent retailer (it's been there since 1852), Marshall Field's boasts a great glass Tiffany dome and an elaborate landmark clock on the façade. Inside you'll discover eight floors of opulent merchandise, men's and women's clothing, household goods, jewelry, accessories, and a choice of high-quality restaurants. If all else fails, at least buy some of the store's delicious, exclusive, and very expensive Frango mint chocolates. *111 N State St, T: 312 781 1000, www.marshallfields.com*

Nordstrom ❶ 3H & p.19
A brand-new and prominent location that boasts four floors and 271,000 square feet of high-end clothing and accessories for the whole family. *55 E Grand Ave, T: 312 464 1515, www.nordstrom.com*

Designer Gear

Designer names thrive around N Michigan Ave, including Chanel, Hermes, Jill Sander, and Burberry.

Christopher Bradley ❹
Bradley's designs are created with American man's sensibility and physique in mind, yet he describes his classic clothes as European in design and concept. *1467 N Milwaukee Ave, T: 773 394 9887.*

Prada p.18
Oak Street's (*see p.21*) latest addition produces exclusive designs for men and women. The prices are exclusive too! *30 E Oak St, T: 312 951 1113.*

> **Who, What, Where?**
> Need help to find that elusive fashion statement? Here's a directory providing all the hot news for fashion victims in town: uncover fashion shows, openings, and promotions, all listed by location and date at: *www.chicago-Scene.com*

buy it

Su-Zen ❶ 5E
This Lincoln Park boutique has something special for women of all ages. Susan Hahn designs nine collections a year. *2241 N Clybourn Ave, T: 773 477 9919.*

Markets

Hyde Park Chicago Farmers' Market ❷ 5M
This is an excellent weekly farmers' market with fresh and flavorsome local produce pouring in from across the state. *Open Wed 7am-2pm. Harper Ave & 52nd St, T: 312 744 9187, www.localharvest.org*

Jeweler's Row ❷ 3J/❸
A piece of history; where lovers have bought their engagement rings for five generations. Here you can find a filigree bracelet or diamond brooch in one of 350 jewelry-related stores in landmarked buildings. *Wabash Ave btw Washington & Monroe Sts.*

Maxwell Street Market ❷ 5I
Moved from its gritty historic home, this is still an untidy but fascinating straggle of used tat, fresh food, and old tyres. A true Chicago tradition. *Canal St btw Taylor St & 15th Place. Open Sun 7am-3pm.*

Spas

Mario Tricoci Salon & Spa ❶ 3F
Just what you need after a day at the shops. Facilities include a sauna and a hydrotherapy tub. *900 N Michigan Ave, T: 800 874 2624, www.mariotricoci.com*

Om for the Home ❶ 3F
An upscale (read expensive) spa that boasts of total spiritual cleansing and a wide range of alternative therapies. *34 E Oak St, T: 312 397 9181.*

Specialty Shops

ESPN Zone ❶ 3H
A huge sports-themed entertainment and shopping complex. Talk, eat, and sleep sport and then buy the

Fresh flowers in the market at Hyde Park

Pretty presents from Silver Moon

T-shirt. *43 E Ohio St,
T: 312 644 3776, www.espnzone.com*

NikeTown p.19
Officially this is 'only' a Nike shoe store. But with five floors, 68,000 square feet, a 900-gallon salt-water fish tank, a video theater, and a basketball court, it rates as something of an 'experience'. You an even buy your trainers here. *669 N Michigan Ave,
T: 312 642 6363, www.nike.com*

Toys

American Girl Place p.18
Shops in the mall feature American Girl collectible dolls, as well as clothing for youngsters, accessories, and a café (see p.45). *111 E Chicago Ave, T: 312 943 9400,
www.americangirl.com*

Uncle Fun ❹
With a seemingly endless supply of toys from eras gone by, you'll find one-of-a-kind merchandise that make excellent gifts, especially if you're on a budget. Cheap, friendly, and wacky is the order of the day. *1338 W Belmont Ave, T: 773 477 8223,
www.unclefunchicago.com*

Vintage Clothing

Flashy Trash ❹
Other funky-fun vintage shops have come and gone, but this lives on. The apparel (from smoking jackets to bags) is quality and there's lots of it. Also a vintage costume service. *3524 N Halsted St, T: 773 327 6900.*

Silver Moon ❹
Arranged by era, with clothes from the turn-of-the-century to the early 60s, and mostly evening wear. Pricey but collectible. *3337 N Halsted St, T: 773 883 0222.*

The Daisy Shop p.18
Picking over these gently used designer clothes may land you a Chanel suit or a Hermès belt: at a price. *67 E Oak St, T: 312 943 8880.*

Paradise for kids at Uncle Fun

chicago entertainment

Chicago is a city which certainly knows how to entertain. Options are limitless. It is as well known for its vibrant live-theater scene – covering massive Broadway hits right down to tiny storefront productions – as it is for being home of the blues, celebrated annually in the week-long Blues Festival. Much of the entertainment on offer is free and in summer, the city bristles with every type of performance imaginable, including comedy, jazz concerts, puppet shows, and street theater. To catch one of these shows, head to the parks or look out for neighborhood street festivals. To stay on top of it all, grab a copy of the weekly free publication *Chicago Reader*, which you'll find all over town. Alternatively, buy a copy of any of the daily local papers; they all provide up-to-the-minute listings.

watch it entertainment

Blue Chicago – one of many venues in the city of blues music

Blues

The blues began in Chicago when southern blacks migrated north to flee poverty and racism. They took out their guitars and settled down in Maxwell Street to play rhythms that captured the city's heart.

Blue Chicago ❶ 4H
A great local landmark club featuring local blues bands and big name boys. *Closed Sun.* **Branches:** *736 N Clark St, 536 N Clark St, 534 N Clark St, T: 312 642 6261, www.bluechicago.com*

Buddy Guy's Legends ❷ 3L
Named after the legend himself, this Printer's Row hot spot hosts premier blues talent every night. Cajun food. *754 S Wabash Ave, T: 312 427 0333, www.buddyguys.com*

Chicago House of Blues ❷ 4I
A launch pad for rising stars and a mainstay for living legends. The decor is upscale and includes musical artifacts and decent art. Traditions include rap, Zydeco, and a Cajun-style gospel brunch served in the restaurant on Sunday. *329 N Dearborn St, T: 312 923 2000, www.hob.com*

Kingston Mines ❶ 6A
Has been grinding out traditional blues for 34 years. Muddy Waters, Willy Dixon, Junior Wells, and the Rolling Stones are but a few to grace the stage. It's the only club that features two bands on two stages

> **Play those Blues**
> In early summer, Chicago plays host to the world's biggest blues festival. The four-day event is free and runs from 12pm-9.30pm each day of its duration. Six stages and more than 70 performers provide the venues and entertainment and if you can't make the festival itself, the month that precedes it (late April to late May), provides a rash of blues-related activities to whet your appetite. Concerts are in Grant Park (❷ 3J-3L). *www.ci.chi.il.us*

every night of the year. *Open Mon-Fri & Sun 8pm-4am, Sat 8pm-5am. 2548 N Halsted St, T: 773 477 4646, www.kingstonmines.com*

New Checkerboard Lounge ❷ 5M
One of the oldest establishments for true Chicago blues in the proper tradition. Now in a new location, it was once owned by Buddy Guy and Junior Wells. *5201 S Harper Ct, T: 773 684 1472.*

Making music at the Chicago Blues Fest

Cinema

As well as venues offering first-run Hollywood films, Chicago has no shortage of arty filmhouses where you can view experimental and indie films from around the world. For full listings, including unusual venues and informed reviews, pick up the Chicago Reader (*see p.61*) or go to *www.chicagoreader.com*

Facets Cinémathèque ❹
Two smallish theaters, of which one seats 125 and the other an intimate 35. Both are purveyors of art films and tickets are a couple of bucks below the standard. *1517 W Fullerton Ave, T: 773 281 9075, www.facets.org*

Gene Siskel Film Center ❷ 4I
Part of the School of the Art Institute of Chicago. Assures carefully curated art films shown in high-level facilities. *164 N State St btw Lake and Randolph, T: 312 846 2800, www.artic.edu/webspaces/siskelfilmcenter*

Music Box Theatre ❹
A wonderfully grand old pipe organ

The retro façade of the Music Box Theatre

is played as pre-show entertainment to get you in the mood. Just like the old days, apart from the line-up of edgy films. *3733 N Southport St, T: 773 871 6604, www.musicboxtheatre.com*

Navy Pier Imax Theatre ❶ 1H
3-D and PSE digital sound for the maximum in cinematic pleasure. *700 E Grand Ave, T: 312 595 5MAX, www.imax.com/chicago*

watch it

The elegant interior of the Civic Opera House

Classical Music

Grant Park Music Festival ❷ 3I
During the summer, Millennium Park plays host to free music concerts, with choral music, jazz, opera or songs from the musicals starting at 6.30pm daily. *Jay Pritzker Pavilion, Millennium Park, T: 312 742 7638, www.grantparkmusicfestival.com*

Chicago a cappella
Stages shows year-round at various locations. *T: 773 755 1628, www.chicagoacappella.org*

Chicago Symphony Orchestra ❷ 3J
Their regular season includes more than 100 performances. During the summer months the Orchestra can be seen at Ravinia Festival (see p.59). *Symphony Center, 220 S Michigan Ave, T: 312 294 3000, www.cso.org*

Lyric Opera of Chicago ❷ 5J
The recently renovated Civic Opera House is the home of the esteemed Lyric Opera. *Sep-Mar. 20 N Wacker Dr, T: 312 332 2244, www.lyricopera.org*

Music of the Baroque
Performs at different locations through the year. *T: 312 551 1414, www.baroque.org*

Clubs & Lounge Bars

Although Chicago's jazz and blues scene is its crowning glory, every other conceivable musical interest is also represented in town.

10-pin Bowling Lounge ❶ 4H
Drinking, tasty dining, posing and bowling: the perfect combination. Next to the House of Blues (see p.28). *330 N State St, T: 312 644 0300, www.10pinchicago.com*

Jilly's ❶ 3F
Everything from Frank Sinatra to Rod Stewart; the Retro Club downstairs is a good place to dance the night

Get on down to Jilly's Piano Bar and Retro Club

Retro chic is all the rage at Liar's Club

away. Next to the Sutton Place hotel. *1007 N Rush St, T: 312 664 1001, www.jillyschicago.com*

Liar's Club ❹

Old-skool punk and glam nightly. *1665 W Fullerton Ave, T: 773 665 1110.*

Signature Lounge ❶3F

The view from the 96th floor of the John Hancock Tower (*see p.8*) spans four states. Live jazz on Sundays. *875 N Michigan Ave, T: 312 787 7230, www.signatureroom.com*

Comedy & Cabaret

Like deep-dish pizza, comedy is a classic Chicago dish: without the weight gain.

The Baton Show Lounge ❶4H

For the best in gender-bending cabaret, the Baton is a must. *Shows three times a night Wed-Sun. 436 N Clark St, T: 312 644 5269, www.thebatonshowlounge.com*

Second City ❶4D

Has been staging improvisational and socio-political satire since 1959. This was the training ground for a string of famous actors, writers, and directors. *Piper's Alley at 1616 N Wells St, T: 312 337 3992, www.secondcity.com*

Too Much Light Makes the Baby Go Blind ❹

The Neo-Futurists rely on speed and chance as they perform 30 plays in 60 seconds in 'the grand Italian tradition.' Programs change weekly and new scripts are performed depending on the audience's roll of a die. *Open Fri-Sat 11.30pm, Sun 7pm. 5153 N Ashland St, T: 773 275 5255, www.neofuturists.org*

Discounted Admissions
To catch a flick for five dollars, head for the cinema anytime before 6pm on weekdays, or to the first showing of the day on Saturday and Sunday.

Drag yourself to The Baton Show Lounge

watch it

Zanies ❶ 4D
Another famous club where comedians like Jay Leno have been flexing their comic muscles for the past 25 years. Several shows nightly. *Open Tue-Sun from 6pm. 1548 N Wells St, T: 312 337 4027, www.zanies.com*

Dance

As home to the prestigious Dance Center of Columbia College (*1306 S Michigan Ave, www.dancecenter.org*), one of the country's finest academies, Chicago has been host to a wealth of dance companies. For a complete list of performances, contact the Chicago Dance and Music Alliance, *410 S Michigan Ave, T: 312 987 9296, chicagoperformances.org*

Hubbard Street Dance Chicago
A long track-record and a broad scope in modern jazz productions puts Hubbard Street center stage as one of Chicago's finest dance troupes. *T: 312 850 9744, www.hubbardstreetdance.com*

Joffrey Ballet of Chicago
Dedicated to bringing distinctively American ballet to the stage, while enjoying a worldwide reach. Ballet fans should not miss a performance by this highly-regarded company. Various locations. *T: 312 902 1500, www.joffrey.com*

Live Music

Alternative, Rock, & Pop

In addition to the blues (*see pp.28-29*), there is no shortage of venues in which to bump to music in Chicago. For large arenas like the United or Tweeter Centers, Riviera, or Park West, book through Ticketmaster, *T: 312 559 1212*.

Double Door ❹
The space is small but the bookings are big. Established or up-and-coming alternative rock acts. *1572 N Milwaukee St, T: 773 489 3160, www.doubledoor.com*

The Empty Bottle ❹
Hosts the Chicago Reader's 'Critic's Choice' bands. *1035 N Western St, T: 773 276 3600, www.emptybottle.com*

Metro/The Smart Bar ❹
Everything from Smashing Pumpkins

Jazz it Up
If you're lucky enough to be heading to Chicago at the end of August, taking in one or more of the performances that make up Jazz Fest is a must. There are three stages in Grant Park (❷ 3J-3L). At the Petrillo Music Shell at Jackson and Columbus (❷ 3J), large-scale nightly gigs take place, while the weekend's sunny afternoons are filled with cozier, more informal shows at the Jazz on Jackson stage (❷ 3K). For concerts for kids, make a beeline for the Jazz & Heritage Family Stage, south of Jackson near the Rose Garden (❷ 3K). Info: *www.jazzinstituteofchicago.org*

Chicago Bears ❹
During the renovation of their home stadium, they are playing at the Memorial Stadium, 1402 S 1st St, Champaign, T: 312 559 1212, www.chicagobears.com

The Wildcats ❹
Northwestern University Big Ten conference member.
nusports.collegesports.com

Horse Racing

Arlington Park Race Course ❹
Jun-Oct Wed-Sun; gates open 11am. 2200 W Euclid Ave, Arlington Heights, T: 847 385 7500, www.arlingtonpark.com

Maywood Park Racetrack ❹
World-class racing just 20 minutes from downtown. *8600 W North Ave, T: 708 343 4800, www.maywoodpark.com*

Pool, Billiards, & Bowling

The Corner Pocket ❶6A
A friendly neighborhood bar and pool hall. Nine pool tables and a

On the lakefront cycle path at Oak St

small menu. *Open Mon-Fri 4pm-2am, Sat 12pm-3am, Sun 4pm-1am. 2610 N Halsted St, T: 773 281 0050.*

Seven Ten Lounge ❹
Eight bowling lanes and six pool tables in an Art Deco-inspired room. Includes a bar and restaurant, seven TV screens and a smattering of video arcade games. *Mon-Wed 5pm-12am, Sat 12pm-3am, Thu-Fri 5pm-2am, Sun 12pm–12am. 2747 N Lincoln Ave, T: 773 549 2695.*

Southport Lanes & Billiards ❹
Chicago's only remaining hand-set bowling alleys. Only four lanes,

so be prepared to wait. Pool tables and an antique bar complete the timeworn charm. *Open Mon-Fri 4pm-2am, Sat 12pm-3am, Sun 12pm-1am. 3325 N Southport Ave, T: 773 472 1601.*

Sailing

Chicago Yacht Club ❷2J
Sailing lessons, rentals, charters, and racing all take place in a marina bordering Grant Park. *400 E Monroe St, T: 312 861 7777, www.chicagoyachtclub.com*

Grandstand at Arlington Park Race Course

watch it

chicago places to eat and drink

Cuisine in Chicago is definitely a buyer's market, with a menu of restaurants as vast and varied as the city itself. From upscale eateries to down-home joints, all-American fare to global flavors, new arrivals dot the boulevards and by-ways in a procession hungry to please the adventuresome populace. With the advent of the celebrity chef, personality counts for as much as creativity, and checking out one of the city's chef darlings, Rick Bayless, is a must. He is king of the most imaginative of Mexican food at his two Clark Street restaurants; and there are several other prominent chefs treading close behind him.

taste it places to eat and drink

taste it

Price Guide Per Person
$ cheap (under $20)
$$ moderate ($20-30)
$$$ expensive ($30-50)
$$$$ very expensive ($50+)

Breakfast

The Bongo Room $ ❹
The basics elevated to the sublime. Try lemon pancakes with raspberry syrup or fine omelets with unexpected ingredients. Great music serves as a backdrop. *Open Mon-Fri 9am-3.30pm, Sat-Sun 9.30am-2.30pm. 1470 N Milwaukee Ave, T: 773 489 0690.*

Inside The Bongo Room at Wicker Park

The Breakfast Club $ ❹
Serving sumptuous and sophisticated breakfasts in an elegant West Side dining room. Treat yourself to avocado omelet, cream cheese, and bacon. *Open Mon-Fri 6.30am-3pm, Sat & Sun 7am-3pm. 1381 W Hubbard St, T: 312 666 3166.*

Lou Mitchell's $ ❷ 5K
More than 1,200 customers daily since 1923 can't be wrong. A real Chicago breakfast institution with omelet and waffle staples. An express branch is found at O'Hare airport (see p.50). *Open Mon-Sat 5.30am-3pm, Sun 7am-3pm. 565 W Jackson Blvd, T: 312 939 3111.*

Toast $ ❶ 6B
The name of this restaurant only hints at its contemporary breakfast spread, which features sinful stuffed French toast. *Open daily 8am-3pm. 746 W Webster Ave, T: 773 935 5600.*

Brunch

Furama Restaurant $ ❹
75 varieties of dim sum are paraded

The fantasy interior at Hillary's Urban Eatery

through this busy restaurant, ready to be selected straight from their steam baskets. *4936 N Broadway St, T: 773 271 1161.*

Hillary's Urban Eatery $ ❹
American food with a Latin twist. Sit at a table or enjoy the delightful food counter. The weekend brunch draws crowds. *Closed Tue. 1630 W Division St, T: 773 235 4327.*

Ritz-Carlton $$$$ ❶ 3G
An atmosphere of genteel restraint and the very finest of French cuisine. Where la toute Chicago is seen come Sunday. *Open for brunch Sun, two sittings: 10.30am & 1pm.*
160 E Pearson St at Water Tower Place, T: 312 573 5223.

Chicago Pizza

Bricks $$ ❶ 5C
Salads, drinks, garlic bread, and delicious pizzas with a variety of eight toppings; try the Brickhouse (with pureed artichoke) and a hefty

> **Tipping Tricks**
> The standard rate is 15-20 percent, which can be roughly calculated by doubling the 8.75 percent tax to equal 17.5 percent. Most restaurants will tack on a service charge when parties of six or more are eating. They don't always mention it, so check the total to avoid double tipping.

Dining al fresco at Pizzeria Uno

house salad. *Closed Tue. 1909 N Lincoln Ave, T: 312 255 0851.*

Chicago Pizza & Oven Grinder $ ❷ 4J
Turns Chicago-style pizza on its head: 'pizza pot pies' are made in a bowl with the cheese on top and then baked and flipped over at the table. *22 N Clark St, T: 773 248 2570, www.chicagopizzaandovengrinder.com*

Pizzeria Uno & Due $ p.19
Established in 1943, these two venues face each other across the street and define Chicago deep-dish pizzas. Go for the tasty midday priority lunch experience of deep-dish or thin-crust pizzas. Also an on-line order service. **Branches:** *Uno, 29 E Ohio St, T: 312 321 1000; Due, 619 N Wabash Ave, T: 312 943 2400, www.unos.com*

taste it

Classic Chicago

Walnut Room $ ❷ 4J
Serving traditional Midwestern fare since 1907. Dine beneath 'The Great Tree' at Christmas. *Open daily 11am-4pm. 11 N State St, T: 312 781 4191.*

Billy Goat Tavern $ ❶ 3H
A popular joint for local journos. The wacky Greek owners have become spoof-fodder for *Saturday Night Live*. *Open daily 6am-2am. 430 N Michigan Ave, T: 312 222 1525, www.billygoattavern.com*

Down the bar at the Billy Goat Tavern

Schnitzel and beer at Chicago Brauhaus

Ethnic

Chicago Brauhaus $ ❹
A mainstay in the historically German Lincoln Square for more than 30 years. Good food accompanied by singing, dancing, and merriment. *4732 N Lincoln Ave, T: 773 784 4444, www.chicagobrauhaus.com*

Club Lago $ ❶ 5G
Celebrating its 50th anniversary in the newly trendy River North area, the traditional northern Italian fare on the menu is great value. *331 W Superior St, T: 312 951 2849.*

Bar at Club Lago

Kiki's Bistro $$ ❶ 5F
French country classics like steak, pommes frites, and pâté terrines are served here; the atmosphere is as cozy as it is charming. *Closed Sun. 900 N Franklin St, T: 312 335 5454, www.kikisbistro.com*

Tibet Café $ ❹
A modest little place decorated with Tibetan artifacts and a large photo of the Dalai Lama. The food is simple, fresh, and wholesome, with tasty options for vegetarians. *3913 N Sheridan St, Lakeview/Wrigleyville, T: 773 281 6666.*

One of the swankier Indian venues on the cardamom-scented Devon Ave. All the delicious dishes like tandoori chicken are present as well as mouth-watering vegetarian dishes.
2536 W Devon Ave, T: 773 338 2143, www.tiffinrestaurant.com

Wishbone $ ❷ 6J
Smooth Southern comfort food like Hoppin' John, tasty greens, and jalepeno-flavored cornbread. Three brothers run the place, with whimsical artwork painted by mom. *Closed Mon. 1001 W Washington Blvd, T: 312 850 2663, www.wishbonechicago.com*

Fine Dining

Arun's $$$$ ❹
No printed menu but the artful, multi-course Thai cuisine is like nothing you will have tasted or seen. Try the 'picturesque golden baskets', which are flower-shaped dumplings presented in ornate baskets carved from vegetables. Reservations required. *Closed Mon. 4156 N Kedzie Ave, T: 773 539 1909, www.arunsthai.com*

Chef Jean Joho attends his guests at Everest

Blackbird $$$ ❷ 5J
The contemporary American cuisine here is all pared-down minimalism to match the restaurant's interior. On a recent visit to Chicago, celebrity chef Anthony Bourdain called this his hands-down favorite restaurant. *Closed Sun. 619 W Randolph St, T: 312 715 0708, www.blackbirdrestaurant.com*

Everest $$$$ ❷ 4K
Fine French dining on the 40th floor prepared by the esteemed chef Jean Joho, who claims to have 'the largest Alsatian wine list on the continent.' The stately atmosphere resembles an urbanite's Versailles. *Closed Sun & Mon. 1 Financial Pl, 440 S LaSalle St, T: 312 663 8920, www.everestrestaurant.com*

Frontera Grill & Topolobampo $$$$ ❶ 4H
These next-door neighbours are run

taste it

by TV chef Rick Bayless. With an upmarket slant on Tex-Mex grub, including some regional specialties, queues at Frontera can be long, whilst Topolobampo accepts reservations but is expensive!
Both closed Mon. 445 N Clark St, T: 312 661 1434.

Fusion

Mirai Sushi $$$ ❹
Despite the name there's more to Mirai than just raw fish. Trendy-chic in presentation and preparation, daily game offerings, monkfish foie gras and, yes, sushi, are all on offer. The upstairs lounge features excellent club music.
2020 W Division St, T: 773 862 8500, www.miraisushi.com

Moto $$$$ ❷ 6l
Proclaimed as a 'technological revolution', with sensory-stimulating fusion cuisine and a magical presentation style, this minimalist restaurant is pricey, but worth the adventure. *Closed Sun & Mon.*
945 W Fulton Market, T: 312 491 0058, www.motorestaurant.com

Soul Kitchen $$$ ❹
American meets Asian meets French. Tasty catfish and seared tuna sit comfortably next to black-eyed peas and wasabi-mashed potatoes. Sizzling soul food and funky flavors.

Culinary genius Rick Bayless

Delicate design and food at Mirai Sushi

You can see why the Soul Kitchen's motto is 'Loud food, spicy music.'
*1576 N Milwaukee Ave,
T: 773 342 9742.*

Kids

American Girl Café $ p.18
Evidence that kids' food has gone upscale. Children can bring their dolls to sit at the table, and if you don't have one with you, they'll lend you one. *111 E Chicago Ave,
T: 877 247 5223,
www.americangirl.com*

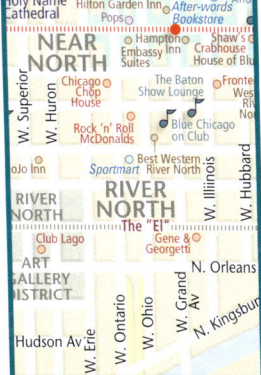

Late Night

Iggy's $$ ❶ 6G
The description 'modern-day speakeasy' aptly sums up this uninhibited lounge, bar, and restaurant. Here you can sup on an eclectic upscale dinner while everyone else is starting to gear up for breakfast. *700 N Milwaukee, T: 312 829 4449.*

Melrose Restaurant $ ❹
The wee hours provide a good opportunity for people-watching as well as nourishing food in decent-sized portions. *3233 N Broadway, T: 773 327 2060.*

Three Happiness $ ❷ 40
Of the welter of restaurants that line the streets of Chinatown, this one comes recommended by restaurant critics and has been featured on the local news. *Open Sun-Thu 9am-2am, Fri-Sat 9am-3am. 209 W Cermak Rd, T: 312 842 1964.*

Seafood

Shaw's Crabhouse $$$ ❶ 4H
This place never disappoints and the annual Oyster Festival in October is a treat. After dinner, head to Andy's a few doors away for post-seafood jazz.
*21 E Hubbard St, T: 312 527 2722,
www.shawscrabhouse.com*

Dine D'vine
**The Chicago Festival of Food & Wine is a three-day culinary extravaganza of fine wines, superb chefs, and great sommeliers. Food workshops, cooking demonstrations, and wine seminars are planned with hourly sessions taking place on Friday afternoon and all day Saturday. Three-day pass available. Oct 2007.
www.chicagowineandfood.org**

Steak

Gene & Georgetti $$$ ❶ 5H
Another Chicago landmark and a good place for celebrity sightings! Prime steaks since 1941. *Closed Sun.*
500 N Franklin St, T: 312 527 3718, www.geneandgeorgetti.com

Chicago Chop House $$ ❶ 4G
Voted Chicago's classic steak house by Where magazine, the good food here is complemented by nightly piano bar entertainment.
60 W Ontario St, T: 312 787 7100, www.chicagochophouse.com

> ### CHIC Cuisine
> River North is home to the acclaimed Cooking and Hospitality Institute of Chicago (❶ 5G). Here chef wannabes cut their gastronomic teeth while practising on a hungry public. *Open daily for lunch, Fri & Sat for dinner. 361 W Chestnut St, T: 312 944 0882.*

Mike Ditka's $$ ❶ 3F & p.18
Decor pays homage to 'da coach,' formerly of the Chicago Bears. Steaks, chops, and, of course, cigars.
100 E Chestnut St, T: 312 587 8989, www.mikeditkaschicago.com

Morton's of Chicago $$ ❶ 4F
The original branch of the famous steakhouse chain in the heart of Gold Coast. Cartloads of fresh fish, seafood, and prime cuts of top-quality meats are presented with a flourish at your tableside.
1050 N State St, T: 312 266 4820, www.mortons.com

Tapas

Café Ba-Ba-Reeba! $$ ❶ 6C
This Lincoln Park tapas bar was the first of its kind and is certainly still the most entertaining. The paella is massive, the sangria flows liberally, and the waiters add to the fun.
2024 N Halsted St, T: 773 935 5000.

Café Iberico $ ❶ 4G
The most inexpensive tapas around and the place bustles as a result.
739 N LaSalle St, T: 312 573 1510, www.cafe-iberico.com

Tea Rooms

Russian Tea Time $$ ❷ 3J
Full afternoon tea service as well as comfort food from Russia.
77 E Adams St, T: 312 360 0000, www.russianteatime.com

> ### Rock'n'Roll McDonald's
> The original Rock'n'Roll McDonald's was a temple to retro 1950s rock'n'roll. After its demolition, its artifacts were all moved into the new building, where they are now displayed in a separate shrine next to the shiny new state-of-the-art fast-food joint. The flagship restaurant features plasma-screen TVs, leather furniture designed by Mies van der Rohe and is completely wi-fi enabled. *Open 24 hrs. Corner of Clark & Ohio Sts (❶ 4H), T: 312 664 7940.*

**The Greenhouse at
The Ritz-Carlton $$ ❶ 3G**
High tea from 2.30-5pm daily.
*160 E Pearson St, T: 312 2357 4154,
www.fourseasons.com/chicagorc*

Vegetarian

Amitabul Simply Vegan $ ❹
Wonderful Buddhist vegetarian
Korean restaurant. *Closed Mon. 6207
N Milwaukee Ave, T: 773 774 0276,
www.amitabul.getwebnet.com*

> ### To Smoke or Not to Smoke?
> All Chicagoland restaurants are now smoke-free, although smoking is permitted in separately ventilated attached bars. Freestanding bars have no smoking restrictions by law, although you may find a place that prohibits smoking in their establishment. It is also required for 75% of hotel rooms to be non-smoking.
> *www.smokefreechicago.org*

The Chicago Diner – the healthy option

The Chicago Diner $ ❹
Wholesome and tasty vegan desserts.
*3411 N Halsted St, T: 773 935 6696,
www.veggiediner.com*

Bars

**Goose Island Clybourn
Brew Pub $ ❹**
Homebrew in a Chicago-style pub setting. *1800 N Clybourn Ave,
T: 312 915 0071,
www.gooseisland.com*

**The Tasting Room
at Randolph Wine Cellars ❹**
More than 100 wines by the glass. Relax on the couches and take in the Chicago skyline. *1415 W Randolph St, T: 312 942 1313, tlcwine.com*

Pret à Manger
The popularity of fast gourmet food is on the rise, especially downtown and in the Loop, so workers can grab a healthy bite. Try the Mexican fare at Chipotle (multiple locations), Panera Bread (multiple locations) for Italian, and Foodlife (❶3G) at Water Tower Place for vegetarian, Cajun, or Thai.

taste it

chicago practical information

Chicago has always been a crossroads, a transportation hub where east meets west. Major air, rail, water, and land carriers connect here and head for destinations across the US. The city's famous elevated trains (the L), as well as its subways and buses, enable travelers to reach most nooks and crannies within its 227-square-mile boundary. The Loop occupies the heart of downtown, ringed by the L. Michigan Ave and its Magnificent Mile flank the Loop to the east. Beyond lies Lake Michigan, along which the city extends for 29 miles, fringed by public beaches. Be prepared for temperature extremes – often muggy in summer, blustery and freezing in winter, occasionally a whipping wind, but with lots of sunny days throughout the year.

Valet parking sign

through October 31. *600 E Grand Ave at Navy Pier, T: 312 755 0488, www.bikechicago.com*

Car Rental

Avis
T: 800 831 2847, www.avis.com

Budget
T: 800 527 7000, www.budget.com

Dollar
T: 800 800 4000, www.dollar.com

Hertz
T: 800 654 3131, www.hertz.com

Parking

There are many garages and parking lots available downtown. Parking for one to four hours costs $7-$20; 5-24 hours costs $15-$24. One of the cheapest is Monroe St Park (❷ 5J), $15.75 per day. *Open 24/7. 350 E Monroe St, T: 312 742 7644.*

Banks

Most banks are open Mon-Fri 9am-5pm and Sat 9am-1pm; some have extended opening hours.

ATMs

ATMs are widely available. Most cards work; many charge a service fee of $1.50-$3.00 per transaction.

Changing Money

World's Money Exchange ❶ 2H
*Open Mon-Fri 9am-5pm.
203 N La Salle St, Suite M-11, Mezzanine Level, T: 312 641 2151.*

American Express p.19
Open Mon-Fri 8.30am-6pm, Sat 9am-

ATM machine outside a convenience store

5pm. 605 N Michigan Ave, T: 312 943 7840.

Thomas Cook ❷ 4J
*Open Mon-Fri 9am-5.30pm.
19 S LaSalle St, T: 312 807 4940.*

Disabled Access

Major museums are accessible to people in wheelchairs and those with seeing or hearing impairments. Most theaters are accessible; for venue specifics, check with League of Chicago Theaters, T: 312 744 6673, www.chicagoplays.com/search.lasso

Most buses and all Metra trains are accessible to people with disabilities. Contact the Mayor's Office for People with Disabilities for up-to-the-minute information about disabled access: *T: 312 744 7050, www.cityofchicago.org/disabilities*

Electricity

Chicago, like the whole of the US, operates on 110-volt, 60-cycle alternating current. Visitors from Europe should buy an adaptor from a hardware store before leaving.

Emergencies

Police, ambulance, fire: 911

Walgreens pharmacy is open 24 hours a day

Northwestern Memorial Hospital Emergency Department ❶ 3G
251 E Erie Ave, T: 312 926 5188.

24-hour Pharmacies

Osco Drug ❹
*2940 N Ashland Ave,
T: 773 348 4155.*

Walgreens p.18 & ❶ **4D**
*757 N Michigan Ave, T: 312 664 8686;
1601 N Wells St, T: 312 642 4738.*

Internet Cafés

After-Words Bookstore ❶ 4H
$8.95 per hour. *Open Mon-Thu 10.30am-10pm, Fri 10.30am-11pm, Sat 10am-11pm, Sun 12pm-7pm.
23 E Illinois St, T: 312 464 1110.*

Biznet Internet Café p.19
$5.00 first 30 minutes; $1 for every 10 minutes after that. *Open Mon-Fri 9am-9pm, Sat-Sun 12am-7pm. 205 E Ohio St, T: 312 645 0065.*

Harold Washington Library ❷ 4K
Free (see p.8). *Open Mon-Thu 9am-*

Public telephone booths

*7pm, Fri-Sat 9am-5pm, Sun 1pm-5pm.
400 S State St, T: 312 542 7279.*

Screenz Digital Universe ❶ 5A
$8.40 per hour. *Open Sun-Thu 8am-12am, Fri & Sat 9am-7pm.
2717 N Clark St, T: 773 348 9300,
www.screenz.com*

Post Offices

To mail a postcard/letter domestically costs $0.24/0.39, internationally $0.75/0.84. Buy stamps at newsstands, supermarkets, and post offices (*open Mon-Fri 9am-5pm, Sat 9am-1pm*). **Main branch:** *open 24 hours* (❷ 5K). *Cardiss Collins Postal Store, 433 W Harrison St, T: 312 983 8182.*

Public Holidays

Jan 1	New Year's Day
Jan 20	Martin Luther King Day
Feb 17 (or closest Mon)	President's Day
March 17	St Patrick's Day
May 26 (or last Mon)	Memorial Day
July 4	Independence Day
Sept 1 (or first Mon Sep)	Labor Day
Oct 13 (or closest Mon)	Columbus Day
Nov 11	Veteran's Day
Nov 27	Thanksgiving Day
Dec 24	Christmas Eve
Dec 25	Christmas Day
Dec 31	New Year's Eve

Public Telephones

Found in stores, petrol stations, and restaurants. Local calls from pay phones cost $0.50. Pre-paid phone cards are widely available from drug stores and convenience stores.

Chicago codes: 312 inside the Loop (❸), 773 elsewhere in the city.

Calls to another area code: dial 1 + area code + seven-digit local number.
Directory assistance: 411.
International codes: 011 + country code + city code + local number.
Toll free: 800, 866, 877, or 888.

Tours of the City

Chicago Architecture Foundation
Specialty tours of architecture. *224 S Michigan Ave, T: 312 922 3432, www.architecture.org*

Chicago by Air
Skyscraper overview by Cessna from Meigs Field. *T: 708 524 1172.*

Chicago Neighborhood Tours
Themed tours, including blues, cemeteries, and literary explorations. *77 E Randolph St, T: 312 742 1190, chgocitytours.com*

Chicago Trolley/Double Decker Co
Hop on and off at will as the trolleys circle downtown. *T: 773 648 5000, www.chicagotrolley.com*

Gray Line
Discover Amish villages and local wineries. *27 E Monroe St, Suite 515, T: 312 251 3107, www.grayline.com*

Noble Horse
View Chicago from a beribboned horse-drawn carriage. *820 N Michigan Ave, T: 312 266 7878.*

Wendella Sightseeing Boats
See the city on a 1.5-hour Chicago river and Lake Michigan tour. *400 N Michigan Ave, T: 312 337 1446, www.wendellaboats.com*

Go sightseeing on the Chicago river

know it

directory

The Chicago CityGuide directory provides the inside track on the 'city of big shoulders', with everything you need to enjoy the city to the fullest. Here you will find a conveniently located hotel suited exactly to your budget and taste. Once you settle in, flip through this section for upcoming annual events (conveniently sorted by season), details of parks to escape to, and ideas for further reading. You'll also find listings of useful web sites, local media, and entertainments magazines, as well as a special feature on understanding the natives.

Key to Icons

Hotels
- Room Service
- Restaurant
- Fully Licensed Bar
- En suite Bathroom
- @ Business Centre
- Health Centre
- ❄ Air Conditioning
- P Parking

Museums
- Toilets
- Disabled Facilities
- Refreshments
- Free Admission
- Guided Tours

Places to Stay

Chicago has more than 30,000 hotel rooms and they continue to multiply. Most are on Michigan Ave, in River North, or in the Loop.

Luxury Hotels

The Drake Hotel $$$$ ❶ 3F

🍽 ❘❘ ⍑ ⌂ @ ▲ ❄ P

Built in 1920, with a delightfully vintage ambience, and overlooking the lake in the heart of the Gold Coast. Dine in the Cape Cod Room. *140 E Walton Pl, T: 312 787 2200, www.thedrakehotel.com*

Four Seasons $$$$ ❶ 3F

🍽 ❘❘ ⍑ ⌂ @ ▲ ❄ P

Palatial and grand rooms with

Price Guide

Price is for a double room.
$ budget (under $100)
$$ moderate ($100-$150)
$$$ expensive ($150-$250)
$$$$ luxury ($250 +)

know it practical information

Tourist Information

Chicago Office of Tourism ❶ 3G
Information on the city's attractions, entertainment, hotels, and events.
*T: 312. 744 2400,
www.cityofchicago.org/Tourism,
www.877chicago.com*

Visitor centers are open daily.
Branches:
*Cultural Center, 77 E Randolph St;
Water Works, 163 E Pearson Ave.*

City Pass
This booklet of tickets allows you to save about 50% on total admission costs, and bypass lengthy tickets lines. Perfect for those who want to take full advantage of the highly notable City destinations. You have nine days from first use to visit each attraction once. $49.50 adults; $39 11 yrs and under. *citypass.com*

Mayor's Office of Special Events
Citywide festivals, parades, and kids' events. *T: 312 744 3370,
www.cityofchicago.org*

Chicago Convention and Tourism Bureau
For business-focused information.
*T: 312 567 8500,
www.choosechicago.com*

Airports

O'Hare International Airport ❹
*T: 773 686 2200,
www.cityofchicago.org/aviation*

Getting into town via train:
The Blue Line train between the airport and downtown runs every seven-15 mins, 24 hours a day. The journey takes about 45 mins; $1.75.

Bus

Continental Airport Express
The daily shuttle runs between O'Hare and downtown from early morning until late evening, departs every 15 minutes, $23/$42 return.
*T: 312 454 7800,
www.airportexpress.com*

Omega Airport Shuttle
Service between O'Hare and Midway hourly from early morning until late evening, takes one hour; $15.
*T: 773 483 6634,
www.omegashuttle.com*

Taxi
Catch cabs outside baggage claim. Taxis to downtown cost $45, plus $2 airport tax. Shared rides cost $25 per person.

Modernist United Terminal at O'Hare

Midway Airport
T: 773 838 0600,
www.cityofchicago.org/aviation

Getting into town by train:

The Orange Line runs between the airport and downtown every 7 to 15 minutes, 4am-1am. 30 mins, $1.75.

Bus

Continental Airport Express
The daily shuttle runs between

Entrance to a Blue Line subway

Midway and downtown from early morning until late evening, departs every 15 mins, fare $18/$32 return. *T: 312 454 7800, airportexpress.com*

Taxi
Midway to downtown costs $30, plus $2 airport tax. Shared rides $20 per person.

Returning to the airports:
Take a train or cab from downtown, or call Continental Airport Express to arrange a pick up from your hotel.

Get Around Town

For all forms of transport within the city, pick up a transit map (*see p.63*) from stations, call *T: 312 836 7000*, or visit *www.rtachicago.com*

Bus

City Buses
These ply major streets from early morning to late evening every 10-20 minutes. Afterwards the

Keep it Straight
Navigating Chicago streets is simple as the streets are based on a grid system, with State and Madison Sts as the axis points. On north-south streets, numbers heading south toward Madison Ave descend, turn to zero at Madison, and ascend again. Similarly, on east-west streets, numbers heading east toward State St descend, turn to zero at State, and begin to ascend again. Numbers are even on one side and odd the other.

Overnight Owl takes over as the night service on most major routes and runs every 30 minutes. Route name, number, and destination are listed above the windshield at the front of the bus.

Greyhound ❷ 5K
Buses to destinations across the US. Departure from *630 W Harrison St, T: 312 408 5800, www.greyhound.com*

know it

know it

Extra-long 'accordion' bus on Michigan Ave

PACE
Buses run throughout the suburbs and connect with city transit. Most run daily every 30-60 minutes. *T: 312 836 7000, www.pacebus.com*

Train

Elevated (L)/Subway ❸
Red and Blue lines run 24/7; Brown, Green, Orange, and Purple Shuttle lines run daily, morning through late evening; Purple Express and Yellow lines run weekdays every 7 to 15 minutes. Regular fare $1.75, $0.20 for transfer.

Metra ❷ 5J
12 commuter lines provide a daily service from downtown to the suburbs and south side. Most depart from *Union Station, 210 S Canal St.*

Amtrak ❷ 5J
Trains to points across the US. Departure from Union Station, *210 S Canal St, T: 800 872 7245, www.amtrak.com*

The L train at Adams station in the Loop

Trolley
Four free lines (Green, Gold, Blue, and Red) run downtown from late morning to evening on weekends, every 30 minutes. Free Trolley signs indicate boarding points.

Taxis
Hail on the street day or night if the roof light is on. Metered rates start at $1.90, $0.50 per additional person, $1.60 per mile. Tip 15 percent.

Tickets & Fares
Elevated (L)/subway trains: The fare is $1.75; $0.20 transfer allows two additional rides on any bus or train within two hours. Purchase Farecards from the machines at train stations.

Visitor Passes: one-day ($5.00), two-day ($9.00), three-day ($12), or five-day ($18) periods. Buy at Visitor Centers (see p.50), airports, museums, currency exchanges and Hot Tix throughout the city. *T: 312 836 7000, www.transitchicago.com*

Bus: Fares are the same as trains, but buses require exact change.

PACE/Metra: Ask at stations, call, or check the web site for details.

Bike Hire (see also p.36)

Bike Chicago ❶ 1H
Rental and tours, open daily April 1

directory

Showboat, this Loop hotel was built in 1871. The exquisite lobby features Classical ceiling paintings. *17 E Monroe St, T: 312 726 7500, www.palmerhouse.hilton.com*

Hip Hotels

W Chicago City Center $$ ❷4J/❸
❄ ♨ ♉ ♠ ≋ ✻ P
Gilded ceilings and inlaid floors combine with an ultra-hip ambience. Their policy is 'Whatever you want, whenever you want it.' *172 W Adams St, T: 312 332 1200, www.starwood.com*

Tax and Tipping
Both a city and a state tax are contained in the 15.5 percent hotel tax that is tacked onto your quoted room rate. A dollar per item of luggage is the standard formula for tipping bell-hops, while tips for doormen are usually at your own discretion.

W Chicago Lakeshore $$ ❶2G
❄ ♨ ♉ ♠ ≋ ✻ P
Look for the enormous crooked 'W.' Relish the goose-down comforters and 250 thread-count sheets. *644 N Lake Shore Dr, T: 312 943 9200, www.starwood.com*

House of Blues Hotel, a Loews Hotel $$ ❶4H/❷4I
❄ ♨ ♉ ♠ @ ≋ ✻ P
Sixteen stories within the new Marina City complex. Original artworks in each room; a mix of eclectic styles. *333 N Dearborn Ave, T: 312 245 0333, www.hob.com*

Boutique Hotels

Hotel Allegro $$ ❷4I/❸
❄ ♨ ♉ ♠ @ ≋ ✻ P
Smack in the center of the theater district, with dramatic decor. *171 W Randolph St, T: 312 236 0123, www.allegrochicago.co*

Hotel Burnham $$$ ❷4J/❸
❄ ♨ ♉ ♠ ≋ ✻ P
Named after architect Daniel Burnham. A steel-and-glass former office building with wild decoration *1 W Washington St, T: 312 782 1111, www.burnhamhotel.com*

Hotel Monaco $$$ ❷3I/❸
❄ ♨ ♉ ♠ ≋ ✻ P
In the heart of the financial district. French Deco design with a touch of subtle color and whimsy. *225 N Wabash Ave, T: 312 960 8500, www.monaco-chicago.com*

B&Bs & Budget

Millennium Knickerbocker Hotel $$ ❶3F
❄ ♨ ♉ ♠ @ ≋ ✻ P
A newly renovated venue in the heart of the action, with a cool martini bar on the premises. *163 E Walton Pl, T: 312 751 8100, www2.millenniumhotels.com*

Radisson Hotel & Suites Chicago $ p.19
❄ ♨ ♉ ♠ @ ≋ ✻ P
Oversized rooms, an outdoor pool for use in summer, and excellent

antique European furnishings and gorgeous views over the lake. Convenient indoor access to the luxury shopping complex at 900 N Michigan Ave (see box, page 20). *120 E Delaware Pl, T: 312 280 8800, www.fourseasons.com/chicagofs*

InterContinental $$$$ ❶3H

Tip-top serene luxury in an award-winning landmark building. *505 N Michigan Ave, T: 312 944 4100, http://chicago.intercontinental.com*

Peninsula $$$$ ❶3G

The newest name on Magnificent Mile; and the very epitome of up-market elegance and luxury. *108 E Superior St, T: 312 337 2888, www.peninsula.com*

Ritz-Carlton Hotel $$$$ ❶3G

Among the best hotels in the US, with timeless decor and oodles of sybaritic lounging. *160 E Pearson St, T: 312 266 2343, www.fourseasons.com/chicagorc*

Swissôtel Chicago $$$$ ❷3I

A highlight on the architectural tour with great views. Home of the Palm restaurant. *323 E Wacker Dr, T: 312 565 0565, www.swissotel.com*

Value Hotels

Sutton Place Hotel $$ ❶4F & p.18
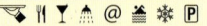
Striking contemporary architecture and luxurious rooms, including deep-soaking tubs, situated on the Gold Coast. *21 E Bellevue Pl, T: 312 266 2100, www.suttonplace.com*

Tremont $$$ p.18

English elegance and unrivaled service. Perfect for a romantic break. *100 E Chestnut St, T: 312 751 1900, www.tremontchicago.com*

Congress Plaza Hotel $$ ❷3K

This ornate hotel has spectacular views over Grant Park. *520 S Michigan Ave, T: 312 427 3800, www.congresshotel.com*

Omni Ambassador East $$$ ❶4E

A classic hotel, which features the French-inspired Pump Room restaurant and is very child-friendly. *1301 N State Pkwy, T: 312 787 7200, www.omnihotels.com*

Palmer House Hilton $$$ ❷3J

Immortalized in the musical

> **Save Some Money**
> Reservation agencies can save savvy hotel shoppers up to 75 percent on their hotel bills. Try the following web sites for the deals of the century in Chicago accommodation:
> www.Expedia.com,
> www.Hotels.com,
> www.Hoteldiscount.com,
> www.hotrooms.com
> (T: 800 468 3500),
> and www.Orbitz.com

directory

directory

and August. Take a picnic. *Free. 500 S Columbus Dr, T: 312 744 3370.*

Independence Eve Fireworks
This festival of lights is held on July 3rd at Petrillo Music Shell, Grant Park, Columbus Dr & Jackson Blvd. Starts 7.30pm (get there earlier to find a choice spot), *T: 312 744 3370.*

Chicago Jazz Festival
Held late August in venues all over town (see box, p.33). *410 S Michigan Ave, Suite 943, T: 312 427 1676, www.jazzinstituteofchicago.org*

Fall

Around the Coyote Fall Arts Fair ❹
Cultural activities in trendy Bucktown and Wicker Park (see p.21), from painting to theater to new media. *Mid Sep. T: 773 342 6777, www.aroundthecoyote.org*

Chicago Humanities Festival
Readings, lectures, discussions, films, concerts. *Oct-Nov, various locations. T: 312 661 1028, www.chfestival.org*

> **On Parade for Patrick**
> St Patrick's Day on March 17th is celebrated with great gusto in Chicago. The effusive and green-clad parade begins at noon on crowd-lined Columbus Dr and heads north to Monroe. At the height of the revels, a secret formula is ritually poured into the Chicago river, which turns the water green.

Chicago International Children's Film Festival
The largest festival of films for kids in the US. Screenings and interactive workshops. *Oct-Nov. T: 866 468 3401, www.cicff.org*

World Music Festival
Music that spans the continents. *Various locations. T: 312 744 3370, www.cityofchicago.org/specialevents*

Winter

On December 1st the city opens up its rinks for free ice-skating. For a complete listing of family and cultural activities, *T: 877 244 2246, www.877chicago.com*

Millennium Ice-skating ❷ 3J
Skate under the skyscrapers at the McCormick Tribune Ice-Skating Rink, *Open daily 9am-10pm. Millennium Park, 55 N Michigan Ave.*

Spring

Chicago Blues Festival
Kicks off the city's Lakefront Festivals in May for one weekend of jollity (see box, p.28). *T: 312 744 3370, www.cityofchicago.org/specialevents*

Chicago Latino Film Festival
Culture and talent from Latin America, Spain, Portugal, Mexico, and the US. Various locations, two weeks Apr. *T: 312 431 1330, www.latinoculturalcenter.org*

Printer's Row Book Fair 4K
Five tented blocks in historic Printer's Row. Attracts international and local authors. *First week Jun, S Dearborn Ave btw Congress Pkwy & Polk St, T: 312 987 9275, www.printersbookfair.org*

views across Lake Michigan. *160 E Huron St, T: 312 787 2900, www.radisson.com*

Wicker Park Inn $ ❹

🍴 🏠 ❋

A quaint B&B on a tree-lined street in a trendy neighborhood. *1329 N Wicker Park Ave, T: 773 486 2743, www.wickerparkinn.com*

Parks

Berger Park ❹

♿ 🖼

Slides and swings in the garden of a large mansion. *6205 N Sheridan Rd.*

Grant Park ❷ 3J-3L

♿ 🖼

The city's 'front yard,' with capacity for 3 million people. Music and arts festivals in summer *(see right)*. *Randolph St to Roosevelt Rd.*

Jackson Park ❷ 5O

♿ 🛝 🖼 ⛳

Has a bird sanctuary, reflecting pond, and golf course. *59th St & the Lake.*

Lincoln Park (see p.8)

♿ 🛝 🖼

Dominated by a Haidan Indian Totem Pole that stands 45-ft high. Popular meeting spot for runners. *Lake Shore Drive at Addison Ave.*

North Pond ❶ 4A

♿ 🛝 🖼

Tucked in a wildlife preservation area. Paddle boats available for rent. *Lincoln Park, opens at Fullerton intersection & 2600 Cannon Dr.*

Wiggly Field (Noethling Pk) ❹

♿ 🖼

Traveling with a canine companion? This is a designated 'off-leash' park. *2645 N Sheffield St. For other dog-friendly locations, www.dogfriendly.com*

Annual Events

Summer

For a full listing of summer lakefront festivities, call *T: 312 744 3370 or www.cityofchicago.org/specialevents*

Chicago Summerdance

A festival hosting free dance lessons and live-music opportunities. *Various locations. Jun-Aug, T: 312 742 4007.*

Ravinia Park ❹

When the Chicago Symphony's *(see p.30)* regular season ends they head north to entertain the crowds under night skies. Bring a picnic! *Lake Cook & Green Bay Rds, Highland Park, T: 847 266 5100 or 800 433 8819.*

Taste of Chicago ❸ 3J-3L

Loads of restaurants participate in this city-wide eating frenzy. There's lots of music and a raucous time is guaranteed. *Ten days, begins end of June through July, in Grant Park, www.ci.chi.il.us/SpecialEvents/Festivals*

Summer Solstice Party

Each June 21st the Museum of Contemporary Art *(see p.9)* hosts a 24-hour extravaganza of music, performance art, and exhibits. *220 E Chicago Ave, T: 312 280 2660, www.mcachicago.org*

Grant Park Summer Film Festival ❸ 3J-3L

Movies every Tuesday night in July

Listings & Press

Chicago Reader
Free weekly music and club listings.

Chicago Magazine
Monthly entertainment listings.

New City
Free weekly info on alternative theater, movie, and drama.

The Onion
A satirical, hip, and funny free weekly.

Daily Newspapers

Chicago Tribune
Conservative leanings and national news. Costs 50 cents.

RedEye
The *Chicago Tribune*'s answer to its longer-form daily is aimed at the 18-34 demographic. Cost 25 cents.

Chicago Sun-Times
The 35-cent alternative to the *Tribune* is Chicago-focused and comes in a tabloid format.

Red Streak
The *Chicago Sun-Times*' daily for the 18-34 age group. Costs 25 cents.

Reading

American Pharoah
Mayor Richard J Daley and His Battle for Chicago and the Nation, Elizabeth Taylor and Adam Cohen. Exhaustively researched story of the power-brokering former mayor of Chicago from birth to death.

City on the Make & *Man with the Golden Arm*, Nelson Algren.
Two books describing gritty post-World War II Chicago.

On the Home Front, Mary Jo Clark as told to Jack Clark.
A writer and Chicago cabbie gives his mother's account of life in Chicago from Prohibition through to WWII.

Boss, Mike Royko.
Hard-boiled journo's astute observations on the Chicago Machine, the Mafia, and corrupt power.

Kids' Guidebook

Chicago Parent
A free monthly magazine, available around town and in bookstores, listing family entertainment. To find a copy, call T: 708 386 5555, chicagoparent.com

Web Sites

www.cincystreet.com/webcam3.html
Log on for live views of Chicago's major sights and fun spots.

www.E-TIX.com
Purchase and print your own tickets to Chicago's attractions and events.

www.Metromix.com
The most complete online interactive guide to Chicago around, covering shopping, shows, films, and museums.

www.WBEZ.org
Log onto Chicago's public radio station for real-time news, music, celebrity interviews, or for archives with audio on-demand.

directory

speak it

So you want to speak like a native? Like any new language, getting the basics is vital.

Pronunciation lesson number one:

In Chicago 'duh' is not shorthand for 'I don't know;' it is the definite article 'the.' You go to duh store; you listen to speeches by duh 'mare' (elsewhere pronounced 'mayor'); you root for duh Bears.

Which leads nicely to lesson number two:

When you say 'Bears,' the 's' must hiss. This is true of all Chicago pluralizations.

Lesson number tree:

That was it! In Chicago the number between two and four is tree.

Here are some useful definitions to help you navigate the city in your new mother tongue:

Food

Sammitch – sandwich.
Polish – a Polish sausage sammitch.
Pop – the fizzy drink others call soda.
Wet – how to order extra juice on your Italian beef sandwich.
Cheese pizza – When ordering pizza all menus list cheese as an optional ingredient even though it's always added. So if you order cheese on your pizza, you get extra cheese.

Politics

Ritchie – Richard M. Daley (the aforementioned 'mare').
Duh Old Man – Alternately referred to as Duh Boss, Duh Mare or Richard J. Daley, former mayor and father of Ritchie.
IDOT – Pronounced 'eye-dot;' the Illinois Department of Transportation, the state agency responsible for all the road construction.

Housing

Bungalow – the classic Chicago-style home. ubiquitous in many hoods
Two-flat – A two-story apartment building. Anything not a bungalow.
Frunchroom – The 'front room' in a bungalow, known elsewhere as the living room.
Gangway – A narrow passageway between bungalows and two-flats.

Getting Around

The Drive – Shorthand for Lake Shore Drive.
Da Jeffer – the CTA 6 Jeffery Express, from the Loop to the South Side
Go-thee – German poet Goethe turns in his grave each time this Gold Coast street name is uttered.
The Ike – Eisenhower Expressway, known as I-290.
The L – The elevated transit line.
The Loop – Downtown Chicago. So-called because the subway loops around the area.
Kitty-corner – Across diagonally, elsewhere known as catty-corner.

A
- Adler Planetarium 4
- Airport, Midway, 51
- Airport, O'Hare 50
- Andersonville 7
- Annual Events 59-60
- Antiques 22
- Art Institute of Chicago 4

B
- Bahà'í House of Worship 5
- Banks 53
- Bars 47
- Bike Hire 36, 52
- Blues Music 28
- Book Stores 22
- Breakfast Venues 40
- Buckingham Fountain 5
- Bucktown & Wicker Park 21
- Buses 50, 51, 52

C
- Car Rental 52
- Chicago Architecture Foundation 55
- Chicago Blues Festival 28, 60
- Chicago Cultural Center 6
- Chicago Festival of Food & Wine 43
- Chicago Historical Society 6
- Chicago Jazz Festival 33, 60
- Cinema 29
- Classical Music 29-30
- Clubs 30
- Comedy & Cabaret 31

D
- Daley Civic Center 7
- Dance 31
- Department Stores 22
- Designer Clothes 23
- Disabled Access 53
- DuSable Museum of African-American History 7

E
- Emergencies 54

F
- Fast Food 45, 47
- Field Museum of Natural History 7
- Frederick C Robie House 7
- Further Reading 61

G
- Greyhound Buses 51

H
- Harold Washington Library 8, 54
- Hotels 56-58

I
- Illinois Institute of Technology 8
- Internet Cafés 54

J
- James R Thompson Center 8
- Jazz Music 32, 33
- John Hancock Tower 8

L
- Late-Night Restaurants 45
- Lincoln Park 8, 21
- Listings & Press 61
- Lounge Bars 30

M
- Magnificent Mile 9, 18-20
- Markets 24
- Marshall Field's 23
- Millennium Park 9
- Monadnock Building 9
- Money, Changing 53
- Museum of Contemporary Art 10
- Museum of Science & Industry 10
- Music 28, 29-30, 32-33

N
- Navy Pier 10
- Newberry Library 11
- Nordstrom 23

O
- Oak Park 11
- Oak Street 21
- Old Water Tower 11
- Oriental Institute Museum 12

P
- Parking 53
- Parks 59
- Personal Shoppers 21
- Pharmacies 54
- Pizza Restaurants 41
- Post Offices 54
- Practical Info 48-55
- Public Holidays 55
- Public Telephones 55

R
- Restaurants 40-47
- Rock'n'Roll McDonalds 46
- Rookery Building 12

S
- Sears Tower Skydeck 12
- Shedd Aquarium 12
- Shopping 16-25
- Shopping Malls 20
- Smoking in Restaurants 42
- South Loop 21
- Spas 24
- Sport 36-37
- State Street Mall 13
- Steak Restaurants 46
- Stock Exchange 12
- Subways 52

T
- Tax on Shopping 20
- Taxis 50, 51, 52
- Tea Rooms 47
- The Loop 21
- Theater 33-35
- Tickets & Fares 52
- Tipping in Hotels 58
- Tipping in Restaurants 58
- Tourist Information 50
- Tours 55
- Trains 52
- Tribune Tower 13
- Trolley 52

V
- Vegetarian Restaurants 47
- Vintage Clothing 25

W
- Web Sites 61
- Wrigley Building 13

Whilst every care has been taken to check the accuracy of the information in this guide, the publishers cannot accept responsibility for errors or omissions or the consequences thereof.

No part of this guide may be reproduced without the permission of the publishers. Published by AA Publishing in the UK. All rights reserved. Licensed to AA Publishing by Compass Maps Ltd.

Written by Rose Spinelli and Anne Scarlett.

Pictures © Compass Maps Ltd and Corbis, Churchill & Klehr at www.aklehr.com, Cummins Photography Inc, Image Bank, Stone/Getty. Cover Images: Superstock, Alamy.

Whilst every effort has been made to trace the photography copyright holders, we apologise for any omissions. We would be pleased to insert appropriate credits in any future editions.

info@popouttravel.com
www.popout-travel.com
© 2007 Compass Maps Ltd.

Patents Pending Worldwide. popout™cityguide as well as individual integrated components including popout™map and associated products are the subject of Patents Pending Worldwide

AA 3258